SNAP DECISIONS

Unleashing the Power of Audibles

By

BILL HOLLENBECK

ISBN: 1-4140-2649-8 (Paperback)
ISBN: 1-4140-2648-X (Dust Jacket)

This book is printed on acid free paper.

1stBooks - rev. 12/03/03

<u>DEDICATION</u>

To
Tommy

ACKNOWLEDGEMENTS

I wish to acknowledge my wife Cindy for her constant love and support. My daughter Lisa, and son Tom, because they are such a great source of pride. The players that made every dream come true, I owe them so much. The loyalists that always seem to be there, Dan Stark, Mike Hill, Mark Ciolek, and Brett Foerster.

I also wish to acknowledge the critical input of Roger Wood and Nick Edson.

<u>PREFACE</u>

The revolutionary T-Reads audible system gives an intelligent advantage to offensive play calling. With confidence the offense becomes a living, breathing entity giving players an unprecedented opportunity for success.

T-Reads, and its support system, offers an offensive scheme that has been cultivated over time and invites cognitive involvement by each team member. When players walk to the line, they approach it with a certain intellectual awareness, and the confidence in knowing that whatever play is called, it will have a great opportunity for success. It gives players ownership, keeps them mentally aware, and most importantly, *"it makes the game fun!"*

CONTENTS

INTRODUCTION

How often are good running plays stopped by simple defensive alignment changes? Offensive coaches often fall prey to these adjustments and can be heard saying "if I knew they were going to do that, I would have called a different play!" What they should probably be saying is "I guessed wrong, again!"

Early in my career I often became frustrated by coaches that stopped our most effective run plays simply by adjusting player alignment. Even though play calling was a result of recognizing defensive tendencies, it was still guesswork and far from a science. **After much self-analysis, I realized that my football team was limited by my own inability to consistently determine the most effective play to call.**

It was with this in mind that I began to incorporate audibles and, in specific situations, give the quarterback the freedom to call a limited number of plays from the line of scrimmage. The results were very successful and the system has been embellished and given a name. **T-Reads** became a simple moniker telling the offense to, within boundaries, "call your own play!"

For years, from the sideline, I would simply point at the quarterback, my signal for telling him it was his call, then step back and wait to see what happened. Our coaches didn't know if the ball was going right, left, straight, or who was going to end up with it. But because of the simplicity of the system, and the confidence we had in our ability to prepare the players, **it was now a science, it was measurable, problems identifiable, and simple to adjust week-to-week.**

The enthusiasm created was incalculable, every play exciting, and our offensive production increased greatly! In the eight years prior to my departure from Glen Lake our record was 76-15. This system is the single biggest factor attributed to the success of our offense, and players loved it!

It just can't get simpler than this!

CHAPTER 1

RULES
OF
ENGAGEMENT

"The secret of all victory lies in the organization of the non-obvious"

Marcus Aurelius

Knowing coaches seldom have the number of outstanding athletes they would like, it's therefore important to establish the most offensive punch possible with average and limited talent. With that in mind, the following statements ring true when it comes to an effective offensive scheme.

I.   Simplicity and repetition are keys to confidence!
II.   The less time a block must be maintained, the easier it is to do it!
III. If the offense can call the play after the defense is set, it is more likely to have success!
IV.   The sooner the ball carrier hits the line, the less chance there is of a minus yardage play!
V.   It is easier to overcome a defensive front if the offensive linemen attack the second level and the quarterback "reads and reacts" to untouched defensive players!
VI.   When the going gets tough, it is best to run your best back behind your best linemen!
VII. It is easier to work with a few players in the off-season than a large number!

It is a belief in these rules that has led to the use of the Veer Option combined with the T-Reads system.

I.   Simplicity and repetition are keys to confidence!

It makes sense that the more times a person does something the better he will get at it. Soon a transition will be made from a tentative thoughtful player to a confident and instinctive one. Instead of being "frozen by analysis", he is free to begin to "think on the next level".

In other words he will focus on what he will do after he completes his initial job. For instance, a back won't have to think about his point of attack, because it will be instinctive. He would be free to think about who tackled him last time and how to avoid a similar fate. When a lineman instinctively knows whom to hit, he is free to think about technique adjustments and secondary responsibilities. As an example, remember the first time you rode a bicycle and all of your thought processes and energy went into keeping yourself upright. But later, when your confidence increased, so did the opportunity for your brain to expand your thinking. Remember no hands and showing off for the young girls? Ah yes, thinking at the next level!

II. The less time a block must be maintained, the easier it is to do it!

Obviously, it is easier to block for a short period of time than a long one. Planning your offensive attack with this concept in mind will contribute immensely to line confidence and effectiveness. Maintaining blocks is emphasized and encouraged, but it is simply not as essential as in other offensive schemes.

III. If the offense can call the play after the defense is set, it is more likely to have success!

Normally an offensive coordinator will call plays that could be effective against scouted tendencies. This is a valuable method, but still nothing more that a guessing game. What if you could take the "guess" out of it? I'm suggesting that off-season and pre-game organization will give your offense optimal chance for success on every play. This can be accomplished by implementing a simple audible system designed to hit the defense at its most vulnerable point.

IV. The quicker the ball carrier hits the line the less chance there is of a minus yardage play!

The simpler the play, the less probability of error. A straight-ahead approach is undoubtedly the simplest and quickest way to attack the line of scrimmage. Very seldom will such a play be stopped for a loss of yardage, and almost never when intelligent play calling attacks the weakest point of the defense.

V. It is easier to overcome a defensive front if the offensive linemen attack the second level and the quarterback "reads and reacts" to untouched defensive players!

An intelligent offensive team should be able to react to post-snap defensive reaction. The best way to do this is to offer options for the quarterback to make. Options become easier with time as player confidence increases with repetition. This is playing smart, intelligent football, and has also been rumored to be fun!

VI. When the going gets tough, it is best to run your best back behind your best linemen!

I've experienced the feeling of needing a yard and not having the best athletes in position to get it. This seems to happen more frequently when talent is diversified in an effort to balance it out. In my case, I feel more comfortable knowing we're giving it our best shot by simply running our best back behind our best linemen. Remember, if it'll work on a short yardage play, why wouldn't it work in the middle of the field on early or middle downs?

VII. It is easier to work with a few players in the off-season than a larger number!

It seems as if coaches are demanding more time of players in the off-season. With weightlifting, summer camps, individual drills, and so on, it's more of a commitment now for a young man to play football than ever before. The Wing-T, and the new spread offenses require more people to be involved in an effort to refine the offensive schemes.

There is no question that an option quarterback must have a high skill level in order to make the offense work. It is hopeful that all position players will make great individual off-season efforts to get better. But if the skills of the option quarterback are in place by the start of the season, a team using this system is well on its way to a successful year.

CHAPTER 2

THE VEER & WHY

"Every plan of campaign ought to have several branches and to have been so well thought out that it cannot fail of success"

Bourchet

As you review the Rules of Engagement it's easy to see why the Split Back Veer plays can be used against any defensive set. It offers an opportunity to hit the line, at any point, as fast a possible. It puts the team in a position where the repetition of a few plays can create an environment of confidence. In general the same plays can be used against any defensive set. It allows the linemen to get by with less time required to maintain blocks. The T-Reads system and strategic player placement can enrich this offense significantly. It also offers the ability to attack the defense at its weakest point with the post-snap flexibility of using the option.

SPECIFIC VEER PLAYS

Many books are available on the specifics of the Veer Option offense. Consider these resources valuable, as they will provide beneficial information for consumption. Veer coaches, like those of the Wing-T, have great variety in their different approaches to specific techniques. For example, the various QB/back pitch ratios and mesh points are always a topic of discussion. Never the less, once you establish what you want your personnel to do, there will always be questions to ask, and modifications to be made. It's like fine tuning a fast automobile, it's never fast enough, but better than most!

I will explain to you what we do, and why we do it. This simply gives me a platform I can use to pass on additional information. As time goes by you will see that slight modifications, unless fundamentally different, will not change the effectiveness of the system. Any method you use to call specific plays is inconsequential, and can stay intact. The plays we review are sophisticated to the inexperienced coach, but simple and distinctive to the knowledgeable veer coach. It is therefore your responsibility to know how to run the veer before moving on to the system that gives it the intellectual punch!

Terminology

Dive Back - This is the back that attacks the line and meets the QB at the *mesh point*.

Dive Key - The next untouched defender outside of the *mesh point*.

Dive Read - At the *mesh point*, the QB will react to the movement of the next untouched defender. If he remains in position or goes up field, the QB will give the ball to the back and carry out a fake.

If the *dive key* commits to the dive, the QB will pull the ball and attack the *pitch key*.

Mesh Point - That point that the QB and back meet as the QB performs his *dive reads*. For the "Inside Veer" it is the outside buttock of the guard. For the "Outside Veer" it is the inside buttock of the tackle.

Laying It On The Table - This refers to the QB technique of squatting, putting the ball back into the *dive back's* stomach and moving it forward as the back attacks the line. This gives the QB more time to watch and react to his *dive key*. This technique gives the appearance of *"laying it on the table"*.

Pitch Ratio - The *pitch back* should always maintain a certain distance from the QB so he always knows where to pitch the ball. If the QB is behind the line of scrimmage, our *pitch ratio* is 2 yards in <u>front</u> and 5 away. If the QB crosses the line, the *pitch ratio* then becomes 2 yards <u>behind</u> and five away. Also, any back running the pitch route should always yell "ball, ball, ball", just to let the QB know he is still in position to get the ball.

Pitch Back - This is the back that is always in position to get the pitch from the QB.

Pitch Key - If the *dive read* dictates that the QB pull the ball, he will then attack the next unblocked person and make his *Pitch Read*.

Pitch Read - If this defender goes after the *pitch back*, the QB turns "north and south" and gets what he can. If he comes after the QB, then a pitch will be made to the *pitch back*.

Outside Veer

This is simply a quick dive with the QB sprinting to the *mesh point*, and reading his *dive key*. If he pulls the ball he will then turn up field and attack his *pitch key*.

Diagram 2-1:

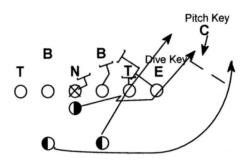

Inside Veer

The QB attacks his *mesh point* and reads his *dive key*. If he pulls the ball he will attack his *pitch key*. Usually, the *pitch key* is the defensive end, but some coaches will block him and attack the next untouched defender

Diagram 2-2:

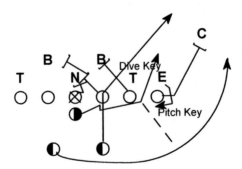

Trap

One of the best ways to stop the veer is to penetrate in an effort to keep the QB from getting down the line. The trap takes advantage of these over penetrating linemen with devastating angle blocks. It creates caution on the defense and has a tendency to keep the opponent from being too aggressive. Simply, the front side guard and tackle will release up to the linebackers, and the backside guard will cross behind the center and trap the first down defensive lineman to penetrate. This is the rule to follow regardless of defensive alignment.

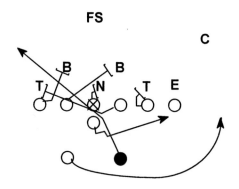

Diagram 2-3:

These are the three basic plays that should be taught, and practiced, until each and every player can operate on the "next level of thinking". Your players should be able to run these plays by instinct. This is why the QB should practice as much in the off season as possible. Once there is an understanding of *mesh points, keys, dive reads, pitch reads, pitch ratio,* and so on, you will be able to move on to the T-Reads system, and experience what I consider "the intellectual advantage".

CHAPTER 3

POSITION SPECIFICS

"Never tell people how to do things. Tell them what to do and they will surprise you with their ingenuity."

General George S. Patton, Jr.

It is important to mention that this system was established as a means of using limited talent in an effort to be competitive. Each offensive position has specific qualifications and duties. As we go through this explanation you will see the methods and reasons for putting the best athletes in the most advantageous positions.

OFFENSIVE LINEMEN

Always put great emphasis on quickness. The faster a lineman can get to his defender, the more effective he will be. Since veer backs hit the line so fast, maintaining blocks by linemen is not as essential as might be expected in other offensive schemes. We always seem to have better teams when our linemen are quick. In fact, often, we've had entire lines averaging less that 200 pounds. A good rule of thumb is that "size and strength is great, but it doesn't mean a thing if the player can't get there to use it." Incidentally, we consider tight ends linemen, and they work with the line every day, all day! The following information does not include techniques used in the passing game or supplemental run plays.

Steps

Every lineman should be drilled on the following:

Base - Short jab followed with an explosive drive block.
Zone - Short 45-degree jab followed with an explosive drive block.
Release - Lateral jab followed with an up field release.
Trap - Lateral jab followed with a trap (45 degree) release.

Diagram 3-1:

Techniques

Every lineman should be drilled on the following:

Base Block - Fire out, fists make contact in the sternum, elbows out, sink the hips, lift and drive. Slide the head to the side you are protecting. Extend hands only on separation as a means of maintaining contact, continue to drive, do not let him cross your face!
Chip Block - Every player works on being both post and chipper with this technique, as it is essential when running the veer. The post blocker should be able to get his head across the knees of the defender in the play side gap. He should then try to get his shoulders in front and hips around. Deny penetration as much as possible. The chipper should neutralize the defender for the post blocker, then move up field to deny a scraping linebacker from being involved in the play.
Trap Block - Short lateral jab, bring play side hand behind the knee, snap shoulders, and explode into target using Base Block technique.
Quick Swim - Normally used as a defensive means to evade offensive blockers, it serves a great purpose for us in a similar capacity. When running the trap we don't want our offensive linemen slowing down the penetration of the defensive linemen. On the snap, if going to the right, hit the defender on the shoulder with the right hand and bring the left over the top, and continue on to the linebacker.
Cut Block - Occasionally the offensive lineman must protect a void created by another pulling lineman. This block is essential in being able to inhibit additional penetration. The lineman will step laterally and bring his near shoulder through the outside leg of the defender. He should then rise up on all fours and scramble into the defender. He should never allow the defender to cross his face, he must go around the offensive lineman's butt in pursuit.

Diagram 3-2:

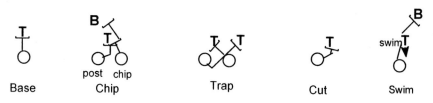

| Base | Chip | Trap | Cut | Swim |

Once these skills have been taught and an evaluation of player talent can be established, it is time to determine position placement.

Flip-Flop Line

Normally we use a single tight end offensive set. This is our preference for various reasons, but primarily it's an effort to spread the defense and yet have a tight end as a blocker. The placement of this additional lineman clearly identifies the strong side of our offensive line. Since we've established where our strength is, we might as well make it that way. Therefore, we put our best tackle and guard on that side also. We call this the Strong Side of the line. To do it any other way is to say that both tackles and both guards are equal. This is ridiculous, put your best players on the same side and give it your best shot!

Diagram 3-3:

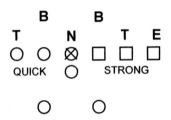

We call the split end side of the line the Quick Side. To make it simple we have a Strong Tackle and a Quick Tackle; we also have a Strong Guard and a Quick Guard. This makes coaching so much easier, and players can identify with each position. The advantages are tremendous and as you read further you will see how this type of positioning and labeling can simplify the game immensely.

Player Positioning

Center - The credentials for this position should be similar to those of the center in any offense. He should be quick enough to fill backside

14

on traps and chip on double team blocks. Since all plays begin here, his reliability in snapping the ball should be impeccable.

Strong Tackle - This person should be strong enough to control a defensive tackle, yet quick enough to get up field on a linebacker. If you're lucky enough to have a better than average lineman, this is where he goes.

Strong Guard - This is your second best blocking lineman. His presence solidifies the strong side of the line. He must be able to drive block and trap.

Quick Tackle - Quickness is essential on this side. Historically, this player earns his position by being quick and aggressive. Because veer plays happen so fast, trailing defensive linemen seldom get to the quarterback. Therefore, a majority of the Quick Tackle's plays are to "cross face and get up field" in an attempt to get to the secondary level.

Quick Guard - This is usually the less talented of the offensive linemen. In some years, with little talent available on the line, we have filled this position with a smaller player without it ever really hurting us. The trap is an essential play this lineman must be able to perform.

Splits

The offensive line must have wide splits. It is important that the linemen be able to chip when the play calls for it, but the wider the splits, the better. Typically we start the year with 2' splits with the guards, 3' splits to tackle, and 3+ splits for the tight end.

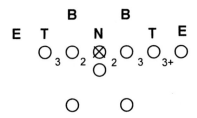

Diagram 3-4:

OFFENSIVE BACKFIELD

Quarterback

This player is not only your best athlete, but he must be durable, smart, have a desire to run the ball, and be willing to put in much time in the off season. This is the key to the machine, when he gets turned on, look out!

Halfbacks

Typically the veer offense is a two back, split set. The back attacking the line is called the *dive back*, and the back going on the pitch route is called the *pitch back*. Since this offensive scheme does not ask the backs to block on a consistent basis, more time can be spent on repetitions, technique and speed. These backs must be able to run through arm tackles. If a back is better in short yardage situations, then obviously he will see duty in these situations. Good faking is essential!

It's possible, but not necessary, to flip-flop the backs with the strong side of the line. If one back is clearly a better fullback type it may be necessary to keep him on the same side as the strength of the line. When you move on to the next chapter you will see how this can simplify the process.

RECEIVERS

Split End

One of the many advantages of having split receivers is that good athletes that may be too light to play in other offensive schemes have a place to play. If you have one good receiver, he must go here. This has to be your best one-on-one threat. The better this athlete is, the more pressure he takes off the Strong Side. Normally when teams use a Monster they usually put him on the tight end or flanker side. This puts the split end in position to have more room to run routes, and evade tacklers after receptions. Frankly, if the defense puts two people on the split end, we love it because that means we are now running ten of our players at nine of theirs. We like those odds. We once went undefeated with a 118 pound split end with quick feet. He ended up being the league's most valuable player. Yes, this is where your best receiver plays!

Flanker

This player is a blocker first, and a deep threat second. Obviously the more talented the athlete, the more he can help the team. But If he's a receiving threat, then his presence will dictate a defensive stretch.

Diagram 3-5:

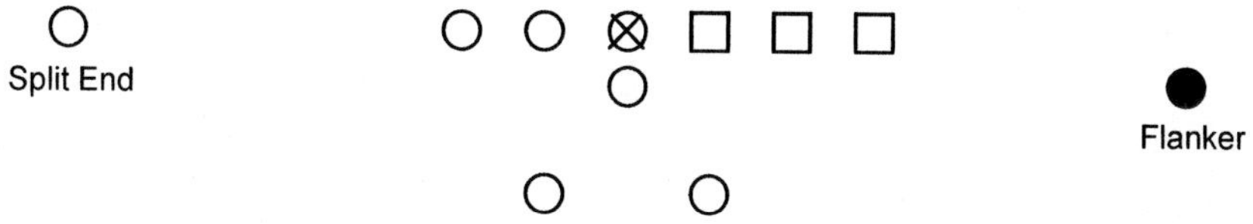

MOVING THE TIGHT END

It is possible to use any terminology to tell the offense which side you want the strong side to go. Our system is the simplest I know and therefore I'll pass it on to you. We always have the strong side go to the right unless we say the term 'TEL' (tight end left). This is as simple as it gets. It is also important to note that the split end and flanker will also switch sides and maintain their normal alignment. All duties are the same, just coming from the opposite side.

This cuts the amount of teaching time because all plays simply have mirrored duties.

Example 3-6:

PLAY OVERVIEW

The offensive team must know how to run the Outside Veer to the Strong Side, the Inside Veer to either side, and the Trap either way. This is all we have to know at this point to make the offense work.

CHAPTER 4

THE T-READS SYSTEM

"An army with banners flying is not as powerful as an idea whose hour has come."

Victor Hugo

At this point we've reviewed specific plays in the veer offense and why they are best for the T-Reads method of play calling. Additionally, a review of positions, labeling, and player requirements has been established. Everything is now in place to start the engines!

This system is designed to attack the defense at its weakest point. It is essential that the QB identify defensive line alignment, it is not important to identify linebacker placements. We call the system T-Reads because in its earliest state, we made pre-snap calls according to the alignment of the defensive tackle. We are more sophisticated than that now, but the T-Reads term has stayed with us.

When the huddle breaks, all players except the QB will go directly to their positions. The QB should take his time and let the defensive line establish their alignment. Once under center, he will use an audible to identify the weakest point of the defensive set and attack it as quickly as possible.

It might be suggested that the defense can change alignment in an effort to confuse, but as you will see, this hardly limits the effectiveness of the system.

THE AUDIBLE SYSTEM

We use a simple color and double digit cadence. The quarterback will start the offense with a call similar to "Set, Red, 42, and then to initiate the play he will say "Go". This gives us great service for what we are trying to accomplish. For the purpose of the T-Reads system, the only part of this cadence that carries any meaning is the last digit. It tells the team which play the quarterback has determined to run. We like using the last number prior to the snap because it gives the defense less time to adjust.

Labeling the Plays

The numbering of plays goes from the strong to the quick side. The first phase of the play calling is labeled as follows:

Strong Side Back   #1 - Strong Side Outside Veer
                          #2 - Strong Side Inside Veer
                          #3 - Trap to Quick Side

Diagram 4-1:

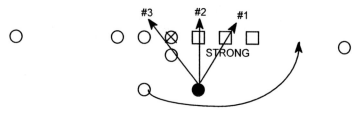

Quick Side Back   #4 - Trap to Strong Side
                          #5 - Inside Veer to Split Side

Diagram 4-2:

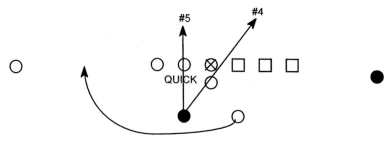

PHASE I

The T-Reads system may seem difficult, but it's actually quite simple. This is when the flip-flop system becomes even more valuable. For example, a strong side lineman only has to remember a few plays. The back on the strong side knows if a #1, #2, or #3 are called, he gets the ball. The quick side back knows if a #4 or #5 is indicated then he will get the ball. The back not getting the dive call will automatically go on the designated pitch route.

Strong Side Outside Veer (#1)

The outside veer is a great short yardage play. Therefore, it only makes sense that it will be successful on an early or middle down anywhere on the field. We do not, however, try to force a play if the situation is not right. This audible system is designed to take advantage of the defensive weakness, and if the outside veer is not there because of defensive alignment, we simply look for a better option.

The quarterback will walk slowly to the line of scrimmage and check the alignment of the defensive tackle. If he's head up or inside the offensive tackle, the quarterback will audible to #1.

This simply means the strong tackle has the angle so take advantage of it!

Diagram 4-3:

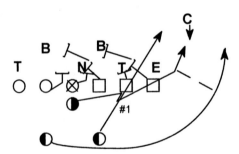

However, if any time our strong tackle can release inside the defender, we go to the next play.

Strong Side Inside Veer (#2)

If the strong tackle is uncovered, it is obvious that he can release to the inside linebacker giving him an angle on a great inside veer play (#2). Any time our tackle can easily release to the linebacker we will call this play.

Diagram 4-4:

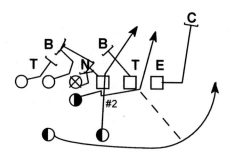

Traps (#3 & #4)

It is essential that this offense be able to run the trap in both directions. The #3 call with the strong guard pulling is one option, and the #4 call with the quick guard pulling is the other. Our normal trap rule is to run the play away from the defensive lineman nearest the center. This presents the center with an easier block, and almost always gives the opposite guard an easy release to the backside linebacker.

#3 - Strong Side Guard Pulling

Diagram 4-5:

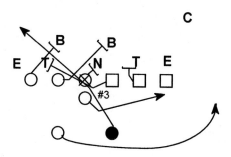

#4 - Quick Side Guard Pulling

Diagram 4-6:

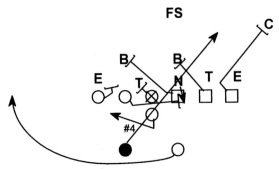

Quick Side Inside Veer (#5)

Any time the quick guard can block the defensive tackle, the inside veer to this side (#5) is a great call.

#5 - Quick Side Inside Veer

Diagram 4-7:

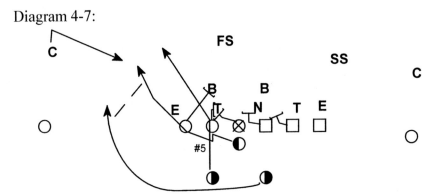

Progression Review

In review, if the outside veer (#1) is available take it. However, if a defender's alignment allows the strong tackle to release inside to the linebacker, run the inside veer (#2). If this is also unavailable, your strong side is overloaded and it's time to look for trap (#3, #4) possibilities. Also, keep in mid that any time the quick guard can block the defensive tackle, the inside veer to his side (#5) is a great call. Please review this paragraph again, and again, to ensure understanding of the first phase of this system. You must understand it thoroughly before moving on to the remainder of the T-Read system.

It is not unusual for the Quarterback to have more than one play to call. For example, refer back to Diagrams 4-3 and 4-4 and notice that a #3 call is also available. In Diagram 4-5 the #1 call is a possibility, and in Diagram 4-6 the #5 call is golden. Lastly, in Diagram 4-7 the #2 call is a seam worth taking a shot at. The point is that options abound and the intellectual edge will provide opportunities.

PHASE II

Quick Side Outside Veer (#6)

Occasionally, in an effort to balance the defensive front we may use a two tight end formation. In this event we want to be able to run the outside veer to the quick side (#6) also. It is important to note that when we go to a two tight end formation, we still flip-flop our line and use T-Reads.

Diagram 4-8:

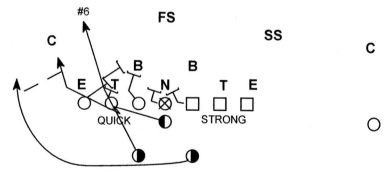

Tight End Pop Pass (#7)

Any time the defense presents us with an alignment that doesn't have a safety directly over the top, we can use our system to run a play action pop pass to the tight end (#7). This has been a very successful play when the defenders decide to change the alignment of the safety. A tight end with speed is especially effective when this play is called. It can happen at any time and will devastate your opponent.

Diagram 4-9:

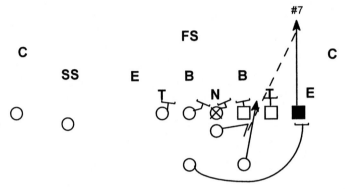

Warning to the Head Coach: "When you're way ahead of a team late in a game, and your reserve quarterback throws this pass against an eight or nine man front, remember he's only doing what you've taught him. Don't give away this great opportunity to reinforce the T-Reads system, simply because the other coach might get upset. It works, let it go, let the players have fun."

When using two tight ends, both will release up field with easiest possible release!

Diagram 4-10:

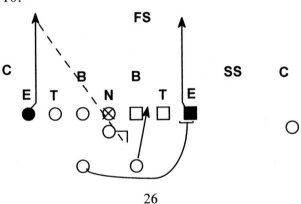

Quarterback Sneak (#8)

The quarterback sneak (#8) is a devastating play and can be run at any time if the defensive alignment makes it available. Normally, the blocking for this particular scheme will change weekly depending on defensive tendencies. We like to run T-Reads in short yardage situations and will tell the quarterback to sneak it if he thinks he can get the needed yardage. There is less chance for error with this play than any other, so run it if it'll work. Again, remember, if a run play works in short yardage, then it should be even more effective in the open field on an early down. This has been exceptionally productive for us over the years.

Diagram 4-11:

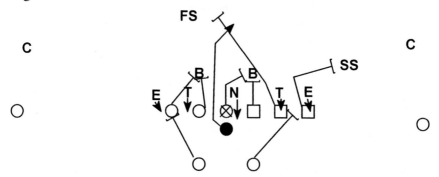

Additional Plays

At this point we've covered a majority of the T-Reads audible system. You may want to begin with a few plays and increase the possibilities as confidence increases. Also, an additional supplemental play (#9) can be added as the need arises. For example, you may add a strong side quick pitch based on the tendency of an opponent to switch to an eight-man front. This slight change could alter the course of a game by forcing the defense out of a deliberate run-stopping front.

Diagram 4-12:

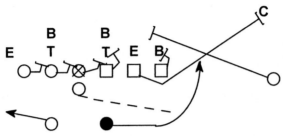

NO HUDDLE — NO PROBLEM

It is not necessary to use a huddle to use the T-Reads system. This is a great tool to use if there's a desire to speed up the offensive series. Using the "no huddle" approach can be confusing for the defense, and frequently results in taking defensive coaches out of the game and may them to use a time out. Another benefit, of course, is it allows the offense to run more plays.

These are all positives and a place and time for speeding up the game does exist. But, in general, this is not a philosophical perspective we adhere to. If ball control is important, then it's wiser to use a huddle and take additional time off the clock. It also gives our players the opportunity to discuss defensive techniques and make small adjustments. If the coach wishes to run a supplemental play, this is his opportunity to communicate it. But most importantly, ball control is frustrating for the defense, invigorating for the offense, and the best possible way to dictate the tempo of the game.

CHAPTER 5

CHECKS AND MOTION

"The enemy resembles us. Therefore, he needs to be approached
as a living intelligent entity capable of acting and reacting."

Martin Van Crevold

CHECKING INTO THE T-READ SYSTEM

In addition to the T-Read system, your own specific supplemental plays can be pre-called in the huddle. If this is the case, and a defensive adjustment reduces the possibility of success, it is essential that the quarterback be able to get back into the T-Read system. This is where a "live color call" can be beneficial by giving the offense an audible key advising them of the change. It's especially helpful for a quarterback that identifies an obvious weakness in the defense. Adjustments made by the defense can offer a blatant opportunity that only prepared intellectual offenses can take advantage of. Should a sneak, trap, dive, or pop pass become available, "hit it now, and hit it hard". The ability to adjust is the key to intellect overcoming brawn.

As an example, let's assume the quick pitch has been an effective supplemental play and has again been pre-called in the huddle. When approaching the line the quarterback sees that the free safety has adjusted his alignment in an effort to be in position to stop the play. Yet by doing so, he has taken himself out of position to defend the tight end pop pass. Assuming the "live color call" is "orange", the cadence should sound similar to this, *"Set, Orange, 47, Go"!*

Diagram 5-1:

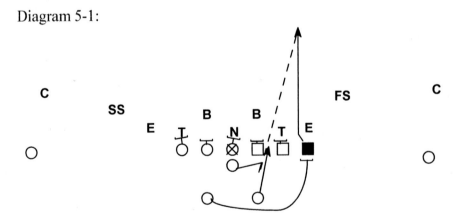

MOTION AND THE ONE BACK SET

Motion can frequently create excellent opportunities for the offense. It may be used in an effort to overpower a point of attack, or as we recommend, force defenders to weaken their position by adjusting to the movement. When we put a player in motion, we have to acknowledge that we have also given up the pitch route on the remaining available plays.

The quarterback must understand that if he pulls the ball on the option he must go up field immediately. It is acceptable to use whatever terminology you want in order to identify the type of motion desired.

"Check Strong"

The quick side back goes in motion leaving the strong side back to use that part of the T-Read system that applies to him. In this case, the quarterback knows everything is still available except the quick side plays.

Diagram 5-2:

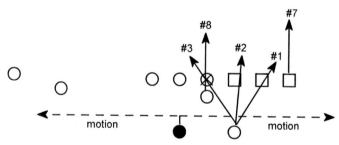

"Check Quick"

If the strong side back is put in motion, the options are now limited to the quick side.

Diagram 5-3:

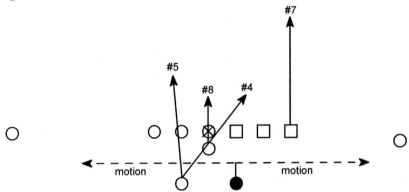

CHAPTER 6

DICTATING DEFENSIVE ADJUSTMENTS

"So in war, the way is to avoid what is strong and to strike at what is weak."

Sun Tzu

The coach should know how to utilize available tools in an effort to give a numbers advantage to the offense. First, however, he must identify the opponent's alignment and the responsibilities of each defensive player. This can be done through film review and experience. It becomes even easier when you realize that all defensive coaches must stop the veer in the same manner. Simply stated, they must stop the dive, the quarterback, and the pitch. After reviewing the opponent's defense it's fairly easy to tell who will be responsible for each of these threats. Acknowledge the adjustments they make, educate your team, stay within the system, and practice accordingly.

The offensive backfield and receivers seldom have weekly adjustments. Offensive line recognition of defensive alignment changes constitutes a majority of the week-to-week changes. But remember we are only working on plays that have positive potential, and knowing this makes offensive line recognition a breeze. With repetition and time, line awareness of defensive alignment changes is easily recognized. Individual players adjust with a full understanding of why it must be done. If you don't change the system, the team will get better with experience. Yes, it's that simple!

IT'S SIMPLY A MATTER OF NUMBERS

The offensive coach should be more concerned about putting the team in a successful situation, than calling the right plays. This means he should know and understand defensive strengths and know how to manipulate them by using formation and motion adjustments. Let the quarterback determine the play!

Begin by drawing a vertical line through the center and count the number of defensive players from this point to the strong side. Defenders aligned directly over the center should also be included. Always include cornerbacks but not the free safety. Since we consider a 3-½ yard play a good one, if the safety makes tackles within these parameters, his strength becomes his weakness, and will eventually get burned.

Diagram 6-1:

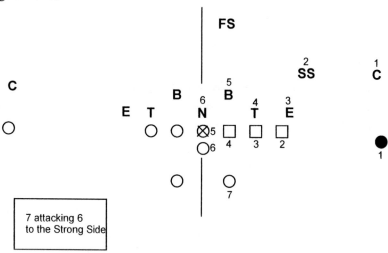

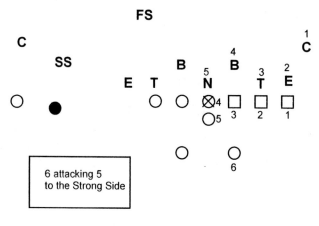

From a numbers standpoint, the Flanker always represents the strength of the offense. Knowing this gives the offensive coach a tool to manipulate the defense. For example, when playing a team using a strong safety that continually follows the Flanker, he can easily be manipulated by formation changes. The offensive coach can dictate his placement simply by moving the Flanker from wide receiver to slot.

Diagram 6-2:

The fewer key blocks that have to be made, the higher the chance of success. Therefore, it's more advantageous to remove the defender by formation than to block him.

Two Tight Ends

Two tight ends usually force the defense to balance across the defensive front. Additionally, designating the Flanker to go to the quick side dictates that the defense will not only balance up front, but must also adjust the secondary to the quick side.

Diagram 6-3:

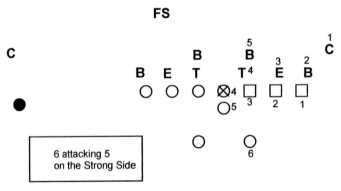

"Check Strong" options as described in Chapter 6 can introduce new play possibilities.

Diagram 6-4:

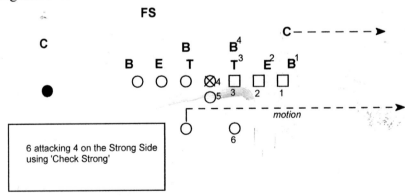

Often it can be beneficial to make a formation change in an effort to surprise or confuse the defense. Please keep in mind these changes are designed to look different, but in fact they are still simply T-Reads with a different look. Below is an example of a formation change that can not only be fun, but also dictate a defensive adjustment.

Hogs

There are many different ways to create an unbalanced line; our preference is to align with two tight ends adding the flanker as an addition to the strong side. Using this non-traditional set, the quarterback should be able to find a "bubble to pop"! The flanker simply releases to the corner and the line does what is normally expected.

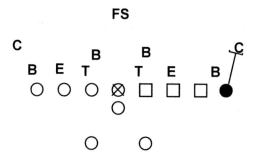

Diagram 6-5:

Motion can add some interesting twists to this as well.

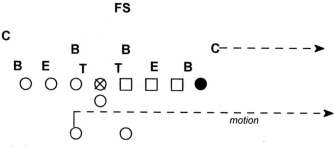

Diagram 6-6:

37

Flex Tight End

Normally when the defense stacks two defenders over the tight end it is done in an effort to create confusion. Usually these players switch duties and at times can be a bit disruptive.

Diagram 6-7:

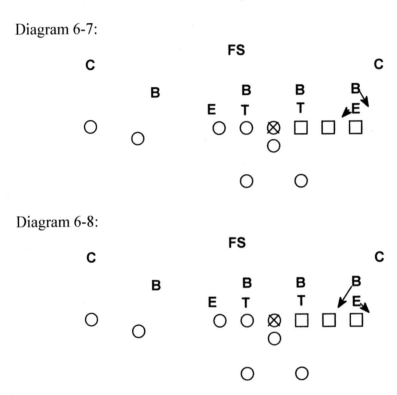

Diagram 6-8:

One way to remedy this situation is to dictate an alignment change to the defense, and this can simply be done by flexing the tight end a short 3-5 yard distance.

Diagram 6-9:

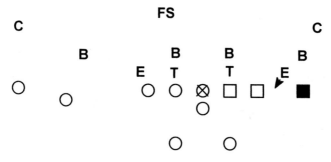

CHAPTER 7

FAVORITE SUPPLEMENTAL RUN PLAYS

"Strength lies not in defense, but in attack."

Marque de Acerba

Supplemental plays are additional to those dictated by the T-Reads system. There are many reasons these plays might be used. The coach may want to get outside on an eight-man front. Most late down long yardage situations dictate plays such as a pass, screen or draw. It could also be the coach's late game strategy in an effort to save 'wear and tear' on the quarterback. Whatever the reason, supplemental plays are designed to remedy situations. Short descriptions of favorite supplemental plays are listed below.

HALFBACK COUNTER

This play is unique in that it uses a fold block at the point of attack. The quarterback will step away from the play, snap his head back to catch the path of the back, pivot his body around, square up and lay the ball on the table. The *dive back* will fake the dive, and the *pitch back* will take a counter step (as if going on a *pitch route*) and then attack the *mesh point*. Against an odd front the guard and tackle will fold, with the guard going first.

Diagram 7-1:

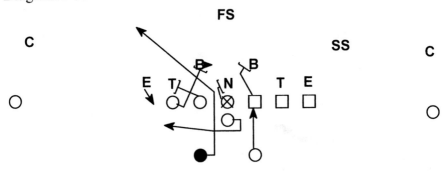

When this play is called against an even front, the center and guard will execute the fold block.

Diagram 7-2:

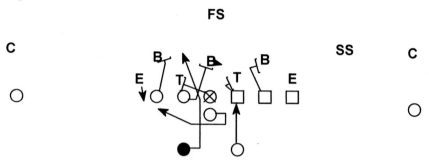

QUARTERBACK COUNTER

The blocking on this counter is the same as the Halfback Counter. The QB steps to the play side, the *dive back* will fake the dive, and the *pitch back* will go on the *pitch route.* The QB will then turn back and sprint through the point of attack. This play works especially well against a team using the free safety to "spy" the QB.

Again, like the Halfback Counter, the guard and tackle will fold block against an odd front.

Diagram 7-3:

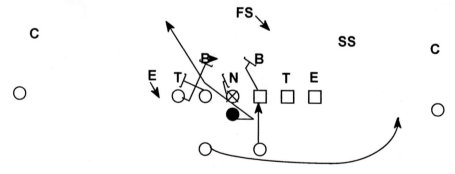

And, against an even front the center and guard will perform the fold block.

Diagram 7-4:

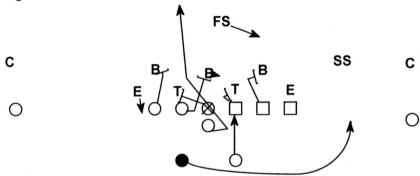

TRAP OPTION

The quarterback will run his typical trap, but will pull the ball and attack the up field shoulder of the *pitch key*.

Diagram 7-5:

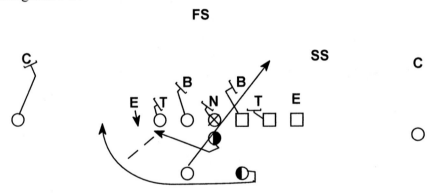

SPEED OPTION

This play is designed to attack the perimeter as fast as possible. After the snap the quarterback attacks the *pitch key* as quickly as possible. This is a favorite because the play is so quick and deliberate.

Diagram 7-6:

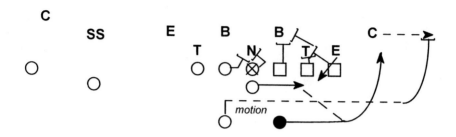

LEAD OPTION

This simply refers to one back leading the other on the *pitch route*. In an effort to give the *pitch back* time to get in the proper *pitch route*, the quarterback takes two depth steps and attacks the defensive end. He begins this process by stepping back with the play side foot first. For example, if the play's designed to go to the right, the quarterback would step "right, left, attack"!

Diagram 7-7:

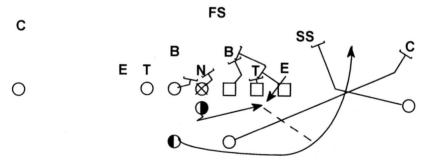

Like all plays above, the lead option can also be run to the quick side.

Diagram 7-8:

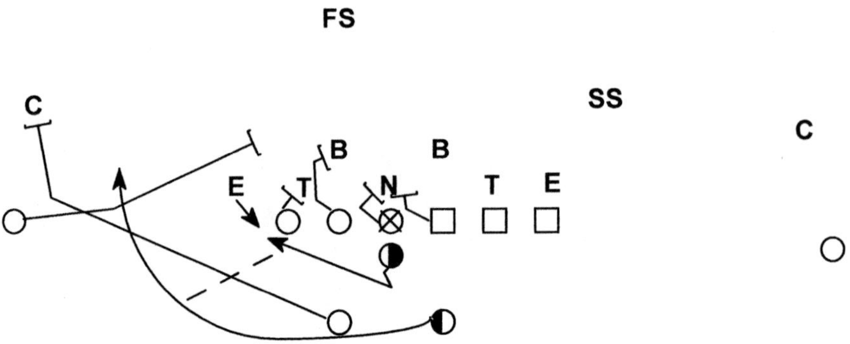

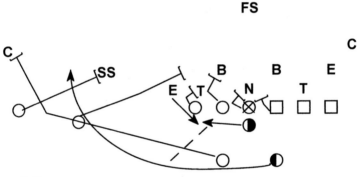

Using the slot formation and a double crack block can also be a very effective play.

Diagram 7-9:

OVERVIEW

Additional plays such as the quick pitch, counter trey, reverses, screens, draws, and specifically designed pass plays can be added as the need arises. If you intend to use a huddle and maintain ball control, plan on about 50 offensive plays in a game. At least 60% or 30+ of those plays should be from the T-Reads system if you want it to be the heart of your offense. This leaves 40%, an average of 20 plays, or five per quarter to pull from your supplemental bag of tools. The more time spent practicing supplemental plays decreases the time available for repetitions with T-Reads, and familiarizing the offense with the idiosyncrasies of the upcoming defense.

The more knowledgeable the players are of the specifics of the defense, the easier it is for them to adjust on their own.

I am reluctant to spend a great deal of time on supplemental additions to an already very effective system. These plays are opportunities for the coach to introduce his own ingenuity and creativeness. Supplemental plays are necessary, but situational and should be seen in that light only.

CHAPTER 8

COMPLIMENTARY PASSING GAME

"Win with ability, not with numbers"

Aleksandr V. Suvorov

PHILOSOPHY

The T-Reads system is committed to a run offense that uses the pass to exploit any defensive weakness. As a defense commits more players to stopping the run, the importance of the quick passing game becomes essential. As long as the defense is respectful of the pass, it becomes difficult to commit too many defenders to stop the run. In essence, the effectiveness of the quick passing game serves as a safeguard to prevent the defense from over committing to the T-Reads rushing attack.

The Box

Except for the pitch on the option, all run plays in the T-Reads system hit the line very quickly. We consider the *"box"* as that part of the defense committed to stopping the initial quick hitting run plays. If the dive and quarterback are not stopped, the pitch is mute. Therefore, the more defensive players removed from the box, the better the opportunity of success.

We can never completely dictate defensive schemes, but it is possible to insure that different areas of the field be defended. In general, if a team is playing zone, the maximum players in the box will be seven or fewer. Simply stated, a three-deep zone with two players protecting the flats leaves six to defend the box. A two-deep zone, with two players defending the flats, leaves seven in the box. Combination players, those in the box with flat responsibilities, cannot do both well (see 3-Step Passing Game). With equal talent, T-Reads should be effective with seven or fewer in the box. Should you see eight players in the box, you are probably playing against man coverage on the outside. It is now time to, "let the ball fly!"

It is important to note that complimentary outside run plays can also be developed to take advantage of eight defenders in the box.

STRATEGY

Again, like the run game, we strive to give the team choices on each play. Listed below are examples of patterns that offer options for the quarterback and receivers. A review of these simple patterns can offer an idea of what a simple, yet versatile, passing game can accomplish.

3 STEP PASSING GAME

The simple combination of a deep fade and quick hitch can give any defensive corner nightmares. The effective use of these patterns alone will force the defensive coach to delegate help for the corners. However this commitment is made, the immediate threat to stopping the run game has been reduced.

The terminology used in the passing game is not as significant as understanding that pre-snap options are made available. Giving a quarterback the option to recognize defensive back placement, and call the most advantageous receiver route, is most beneficial. For example, when the quick hitch is called in the huddle, it is to be thrown unless the defensive corner presses the receiver. Using the last digit in the cadence, the quarterback calls a pre-selected number to indicate to the receivers that a fade route is expected. In this case, the number used as the *deep indicator* is "2".

Diagram 8-1:

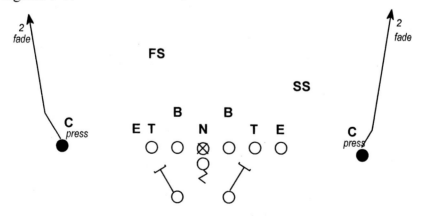

Another means of making a pre-snap decision can be used by both receiver and quarterback acknowledging defender alignment. For example, if we are in a slot formation, our receivers and quarterback will identify the depth of the defenders. The receiver with the deepest defender runs a hitch, and the one with the closest defender runs the streak. The quarterback's primary receiver is the one running the hitch.

Diagram 8-2:

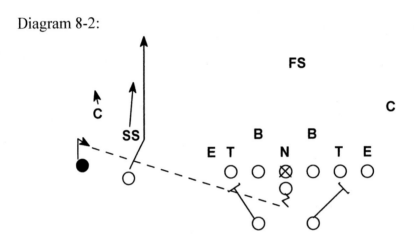

Diagram 8-3:

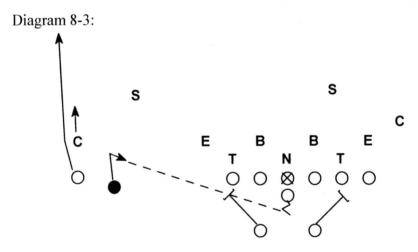

We always throw the hitch unless the quarterback believes he can get the ball to the receiver going deep. In this case, he will use the *deep indicator* "2", and take advantage of the situation.

Diagram 8-4:

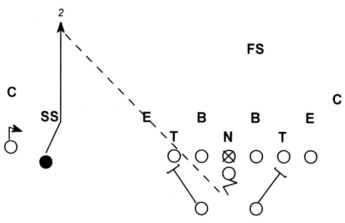

These two patterns alone should force the defense to honor your ability to pass, and insure a maximum of seven in the box. If not, the inability to make completions will also stop the run game and make for a long ride home. This is why the ability to run these two patterns is such an essential part of keeping your offense effective.

PLAY ACTION

In addition to the tight end pop pass, the following two patterns have been highly successful play action passes.

Flanker Fade

If the defensive corner covering our flanker is quickly attacking the pitch, we know a play action fade should be a good play. In addition, when playing a team using man-to-man coverage, we often have our receivers run them off rather than attempting blocks. This keeps the corner from getting to the pitch in a hurry. With success on our pitches, these corners feel pressured to come up quicker and let the receiver fly by. Again, this is a great opportunity to run the play action flanker fade.

Diagram 8-5:

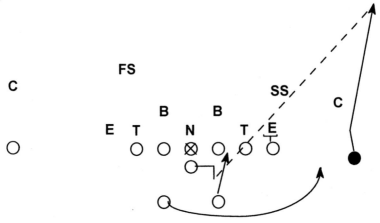

Split End Slant

When playing a defense using a strong safety, and the defenders are putting seven in the box, this usually leaves the split end slant pass wide open.

Diagram 8-6:

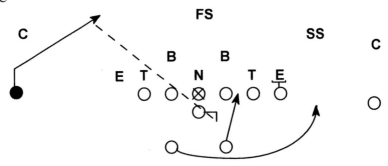

The existence of these patterns will keep the defenders from over committing to the run, and all patterns should be given daily repetitions to ensure confidence.

CHAPTER 9

FREQUENTLY ASKED QUESTIONS

"The will to win is important, but the will to prepare is vital."

Joe Paterno

With an offense like the veer, doesn't it bother you knowing that the defense knows what plays you run?

First of all, it isn't what plays you run it's how well you run them! Hopefully, repetition will create confidence, and the T-Reads system will take advantage of defensive alignment. Frankly, I consider it an advantage knowing the defense understands what they have to stop. This allows me to consider their options and plan accordingly. As time goes by you'll see there are only so many things the defense can do, and you will be accustomed to making the necessary adjustments.

What if the defense knows your audible system?

If a coach is spending time trying to pick up the audible system, he is not using it to effectively to make his own team better. It's his job to coach the whole team, including all aspects of offense, defense, and specialty teams. Not only is this poor use of time on his part, but it can only work in your favor. Besides, if you suspect the opposition is keying on audible calls, simply pre-call a specific play in the huddle, and use a number in the cadence that works against it. For example, let's assume a trap option is called in the huddle. Knowing this the QB should use a number in the cadence (in this case #3) that influences the linebackers to jump on the trap.

Diagram 9-1:

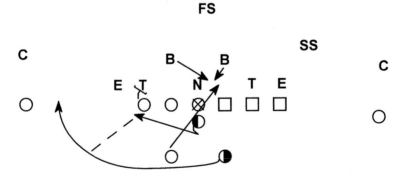

This causes confusion and creates a lack of confidence in the defensive game plan. Now, all the time and effort put into this arguable plan to cheat is lost forever. You have the defense right where you want it!

What if the defensive line moves around prior to the snap?

Rarely has this been a problem to be concerned with. Since we use the last digit prior to "Go", there's little time for defensive adjustments. However, if this happens, run the play anyway and move on. The defense can't do this on a consistent basis and be effective. But if they could, simply tell your quarterback to slow things down and wait until the defender goes back to his original spot.

Isn't it hard to teach the T-Reads system?

Once the basic plays of the veer offense are understood, and the players can perform their duties at a reasonable level, implementation of the T-Reads system is simple. The team needs to get as many opportunities to run these plays as possible, and it should be done using T-Reads in an effort to reinforce the advantages of the audible system. Coaches that spend much time having their team run the same play against every possible front as if to say, "no matter what, we will run this play", are of a totally different mind set. Using this system, eventually, the coaches and players will realize the T-Reads system uses the play with the best opportunity for success.

Aren't you afraid to let go of the offensive play calling?

No, absolutely not, this is the best possible opportunity for success. Players that run this system are not robots, but living, breathing parts of the whole. They have ownership and feel as if they are masters of their own destiny. They are in the game physically, mentally, and with the emotion that can only come with complete immersion.

Knowing that any offensive play can be pre-called, offensive control can still be manipulated by the coach. But I believe there is too much of this, and the game should be given back to the players.

What if the defense switches sides with your strong side?

In some schemes the defensive coach will do this week to week by design. If this is the case, anticipate it, and accept the challenge that your best will probably be playing their best. This is football!
However, if it is uncharacteristic of the defense to flip-flop then they're telling you they don't have confidence in a certain number of players. Also, if this is a new concept it's possible the defenders are not as strong playing on the left side as they are to the right, or vice versa. Lastly, is their obvious weaker group better than the offensive quick side? If all these things are true, you're still attacking with your best athletes, and <u>you've got yourself a game</u>!

How do you communicate desired play calls to your team?

For the complimentary plays we use a simple 0-9 numbering system using our right hand to systematically tap certain areas of our upper body. The T-Reads system is given by a simple hand signal (for five years I just pointed to the QB). Additional signs are necessary when communicating specifics about plays or calls with the quarterback. For example, if in T-Reads the quarterback is not calling a play we think is open, it's important this be communicated to him. In our case, if the coach points to his eye, he is saying, "look for this", and he will then give the number of the play in T-Reads he wants the quarterback to look for. Due to defensive adjustments, the play may not be available next time, but the quarterback will surely check for it. Also, if the right play is called, but the quarterback makes the wrong post-snap decision, the coach may want to let him know. For example, if the quarterback should have given on the dive, we use a fist; if he should have kept the ball, we tap our stomach; and if he should have pitched the ball, we flick our hand to the outside. Often, following a play, the quarterback will look at the coach and signal back what he did wrong, without any input from the coach.
In this case, a simple smile and nod by the coach will suffice. It is important to note that yelling at the quarterback does not help, he has enough to think about. Offer smiles, confidence-building gestures, and learn to live with it!

In your cadence, do you always go on the first "Go"?

Yes, almost entirely, and always when using T-Reads. With all the pre-snap decisions to be made, it is very difficult to change the cadence. We seldom work on varying it and feel this saves an immense amount of practice time. Having confidence in this simple part of the game is a great step for the team to build on. We would rather work on technique than spend time on something that would undermine confidence. This may, at times give the opponent an edge coming off the ball, but knowing we are confidently hitting the weakest part of the defense is much more reassuring. It helps knowing the best traps are run when the defensive line gets a good jump.

We can reinforce this consistently during our own practices. Obviously, our defensive scout team is not only aware of our cadence, but also the T-Reads system. So all week long in practice the offense conditions itself to make small adjustments to "keep the defense honest".

If a change in cadence is desired, it's as easy as pre-calling a specific play and count. This is, however, a time when the quarterback should be encouraged to "rattle some cages" in the huddle in an effort to reinforce the change. To give more credibility to this philosophy, it should be noted that our teams have all but eliminated offensive neutral zone infractions. For a coach that likes to eliminate potential problems, this method has had ideal results.

If we need an offensive time out, and time on the clock is not an issue, our favorite option is to use a term in the huddle we refer to as "Chatter". This simply means that under no circumstances will we snap the ball. The quarterback will attempt to draw the opposition into the neutral zone with a long count. Our team considers this an actual play and understands why we use it. If the defense commits encroachment, the penalty will change the situation and a time out probably won't be necessary. If there isn't encroachment, make note of the defensive alignment, call time out and plan accordingly. Using this concept your coaches have more information to prepare the quarterback to make a successful play call.

Doesn't it concern you that your quarterback gets hit so often?

It is a concern, but in 22 years of running the veer we have never lost a quarterback to injury on a veer option play. We have had injuries to quarterbacks attempting to pass and not seeing a blitz coming. It seems as if the aggressive attitude a quarterback must have mentally prepares him for physical play. Don't get me wrong, this is not a position for a player with a low pain threshold. He will get hit on almost every play and have bumps and bruises galore following the game. He will also have a huge smile on his face!

CHAPTER 10

MAKING SIMPLE ADJUSTMENTS

"Hit the other fellow as quick as you can, and as hard as you can,
where it hurts him most, when he ain't lookin."

Unrecorded British Sgt Major
(on the definition of strategy)

It is important that football teams be able to make adjustments during the course of a game. When coaches do their job, and players understand why changes have to be made, they can be made instantly and with conviction.

Offensive adjustments come in a variety of ways, for example, the essence of T-Reads is it allows plays to be called that take advantage of defensive alignment. Additional changes occur when the offensive coach, through formational changes, creates numerical advantages for the use of T-Reads. Lastly, and the subject of this chapter, are examples of technique changes that can be made when a play is actually being run.

CHANGING PLAY TECHNIQUES

The coach has two distinct advantages when looking for defensive keys and adjustments. Initially, because the offensive backfield originates each play with two split backs, it is easy to determine how the linebackers are reacting to their movement. Secondly, because all phases of the triple option must be stopped, player responsibilities are blatantly obvious. Careful evaluation can result in a small change that will make all the difference in the world. As you know, once the defense loses confidence in its ability to defend; the floodgates can open.

Listed below are examples of changes we've utilized over the years. It is your charge, as the coach, to know your offense well enough to be able to make similar adjustments as the need arises.

The Trap

If it is determined that the linebackers are reading the back directly over them as in Diagram 10-1.

Diagram 10-1:

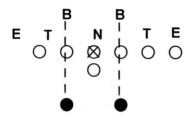

Meaning they are crashing if he dives, and checking backside if he goes away.

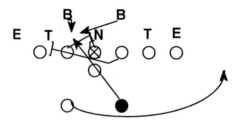

Diagram 10-2:

Simply have the pitch back attack the off-tackle hole in an effort to pull the linebacker to the line. Now the play side offensive tackle can block him.

Diagram 10-3:

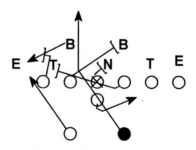

As previously stated, the angles are best if the QB calls the trap away from the nearest defensive lineman to the center. However, good scouting may introduce even better tendencies. For example, if one defensive lineman is big and slow, and the other is quick, it would be more beneficial to trap the quicker of the two. This is a point the coach should prep the QB on during the week. Also, constant communication with the line in the huddle can identify the defender most vulnerable to the trap. However, for the purpose of teaching the basics of the T-Reads system we will follow the rule and only trap away from the nearest defensive lineman to the center.

The Inside Veer

On occasion we'll run into a team that will align the defensive tackle on the outside of our tackle making it appear that the #2 call is wide open. They will then crash this tackle hard on the dive. In addition, they will use the same technique with the defensive end and try to get him on our QB before he can get the pitch off.

Diagram 10-4:

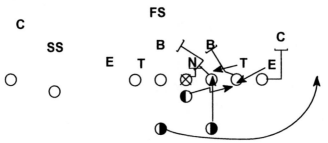

Again, a simple adjustment can make this play very effective. Instead of arc releasing the tight end into the secondary, have him base block the end and let the QB cut up inside.

Diagram 10-5:

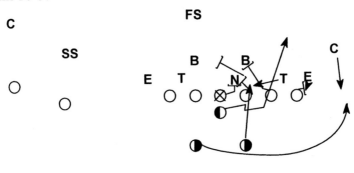

In the event the defensive end still crashes hard, the tight end will ride him and the QB can cut off his butt and attack the secondary, as he would with the outside veer.

Diagram 10-6:

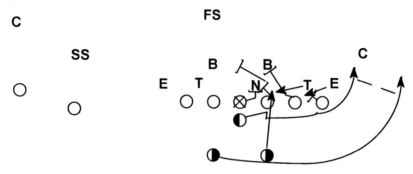

The Outside Veer

Frequently the defensive end will be coached to read the movement of the tight end. If he blocks down the defender will attack the dive or QB.

Diagram 10-7:

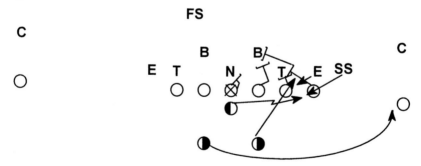

Normally this isn't a problem because the QB will read the defensive end and continue with the options of the play. However, it is possible to release the tight end, giving the defensive end a reason to fight what appears to be a hook block and give up his option duties. If your strong tackle and guard can handle the defensive tackle and linebacker, this play will be off to the races!

Diagram 10-8:

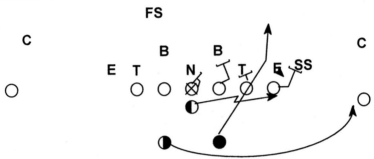

These are just a few examples of how adjustments can be made when a coach knows his offense well enough to put the players in position to be successful!

CHAPTER 11

PRACTICE AND DRILLS

"I find that the harder I work the more luck I seem to have."

Thomas Jefferson

In an effort to keep players fresh and excited we try to run practice as efficiently as possible. A typical offensive segment includes about 20 minutes of individual drill and 30 minutes of team scrimmage. The scrimmage is live on the line with scout players simply 'wrapping' the backs and receivers. Because most relevant T-Reads adjustments concern the offensive line, it's important these players experience constant work. It isn't necessary this happen every day, but it must happen enough to create confidence in the line and with T-Reads in general.

POSITION SPECIFIC DRILLS

Every position must receive enough repetitions to reinforce player confidence in game essential duties.

Offensive Line and Tight Ends

We review all facets of the responsibilities of an offensive lineman on a daily basis. In addition to pass protection drills we emphasize the run game from several perspectives. Initially we work with the players on an individual basis, then small groups, and lastly in a team scrimmage situation.

Individual —

- Steps - Review will be given to the steps described in Chapter 3. For example a coach will review the base, zone, release, and trap steps. These drills will be reinforced and reviewed as often as possible. It must be understood that all blocking begins with these steps.

- Assume the Position (7-Man Sled) - The players will assume a blocking position by fitting themselves against the sled. The coach will review their form (flat back, legs flexed, fists together, elbows out, head up and to the side). The coach will blow the whistle and the players will drive block using this pre-fitted position.

- Cut Block (7-Man Sled) - Align players in the gap, and on the whistle they should take their away shoulder and put it across the far lower corner of the pad. Extend the hands on the ground, work the hips around, and scramble into the defender in an effort to maintain contact. Again, this should be done several times each way daily.

- Drive Block (Chutes & Big Block Dummy) - As described above, drive the dummy out and away. It is with this dummy, however, that the lineman can now work on the two-hand shove prior to separation.

- Trap Block (Chutes & Big Block Dummy) - The lineman should align himself perpendicular to the chute, get in his stance, and on command attack the dummy using his trap steps, explode on contact and slide head toward the line of scrimmage.

- Quick Swim (Big Block Dummy) - Reinforce this frequently used defensive technique to improve the ability of all linemen to release and get up into the linebackers.

Small Group -

- Chip Block (2 Big Block Dummies) - Using two linemen, align the dummies in a staggered fashion. The linemen are labeled according to their duties. The "post" is the lineman that crosses in front of the defender, and the "chip" is the one that makes contact and moves "up the ladder" to the linebacker.

Diagram 11-1:

Eventually this drill can be done without the dummies for a more real effect. The performance of this technique cannot be emphasized enough, as it is essential that all linemen be able to perform both "post" and "chip" techniques at any time.

- Trap Block (Live) - All facets of the trap game must be reviewed constantly. We have two general rules about trapping: (1) Trap away from the nearest linemen to the center, (2) trap the first down lineman past the center. The advantages to these rules are immense. The center has an easy block, the play side guard has an easier release to the opposite linebacker, the trapping guard has more room to open a hole, and the QB can identify his audible calls easily.

Remember the simple trap rule; "always go away from the nearest down defender to the center!"

Diagram 11-2:

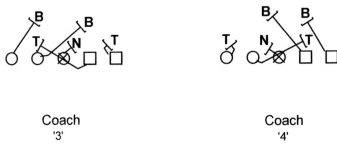

<table>
<tr><td>Coach
'3'</td><td>Coach
'4'</td></tr>
</table>

It is important to run all drills from the 'TEL' formation also.

Diagram 11-3:

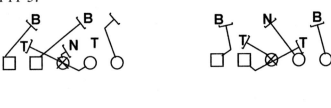

<table>
<tr><td>Coach
'4'</td><td>Coach
'3'</td></tr>
</table>

The coach will make the trap calls (3 or 4) in this drill for practical reinforcement.

Team Scrimmage —

- Team Scrimmage (Live on line, soft wrap backs) - This is the opportunity for the coach to adjust the defensive set to give the QB and line an opportunity to acclimate themselves to the upcoming opponent and the options available by their defensive tendencies.

Quarterback and Backs

It is essential that the QB and backs maintain the integrity of their *mesh points*. As described in Chapter 2 the *mesh point* for the outside veer is the inside cheek of the tackle, and the *mesh point* for the inside veer is the outside cheek of the guard. This can be reinforced in a number of ways. We often use cones to indicate the *mesh points* and run play after play just to get the confidence up. We also place coaches or players in *dive key* and *pitch key* positions to force the QB to make decisions.

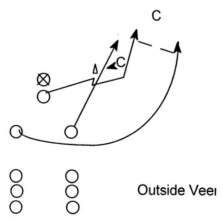

Outside Veer

Diagram 11-4:

Diagram 11-5:

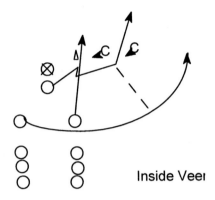

Inside Veer

It is also necessary to reinforce the *mesh point* for the trap.

Diagram 11-6:

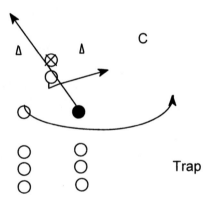

Trap

It is important to note that a snap must be replicated in some way to ensure that the timing is not changed when a center is used. We usually do this by having the QB slap the ball after he completes his cadence, and this seems to work well.

Obviously, all supplemental plays, pass blocking, downfield blocking, ball control, must also be reviewed during the offensive back individual sessions. But this brings to light the importance of not over committing your offense to a great many plays and formations. Again, just be good at what you do!

Receivers

The first technique our receivers work on, no matter what time of year, is stalk blocking.

Stalk Block - With effort and constant reinforcement this block can become quite easy to perform. We have our receivers attack the defensive back quickly and break down about three yards from him. We know he's watching the ball and we make it a goal to stay in front of his eyes. Our backs will cut on the block of the wide receivers; therefore staying in front of his eyes serves us well. The blocker should stay on a lateral plane and punch the defender's shoulder pads with the base of his hands. When he tries to make a commitment, drive back the shoulder on the side he is looking, and force him to run the long way around you.

Our most effective receiving drill has been 10-yard burnout! Have the receivers get a partner, stand 10 yards apart and throw the ball hard at each other. Normally this is a pre-practice drill that has given us excellent results as it forces players to <u>catch with their hands</u>.

CHAPTER 12

OVERVIEW

"The world is not interested in the storms you encountered, but did you bring in the ship?"

William McFee

The following is an overview of most defensive alignments and the play calling possibilities for each. Remember, the quarterback is only concerned with the pre-snap location of the defensive linemen. The quarterback keep (#8) will always be called if the alignment and situation call for it. Also keep in mind that the tight end pop pass (#7) can be called at any time if there is no coverage 'over the top'. The following examples will therefore primarily emphasize calls #1 through #6.

A variety of alignments for each defense will be shown, try to determine on your own which possible play calls are available. The correct responses and examples will follow at the end of this chapter.

4-3 Defense

Pull the strong safety away by going to slot formation

Diagram 12-1:

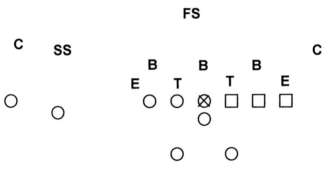

Another defensive look may appear as follows.

Diagram 12-2:

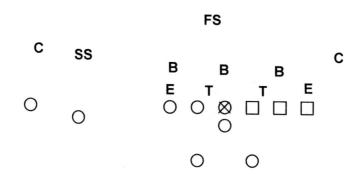

4-4 Defense

Diagram 12-3:

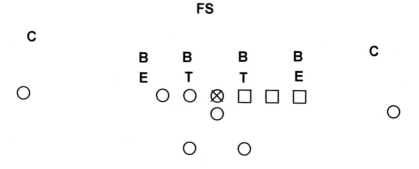

Slot formation can be effective against a balanced defense because it forces the quick side outside linebacker to go out and play on the slot. This clearly weakens the inside pursuit of this defender.

Diagram 12-4:

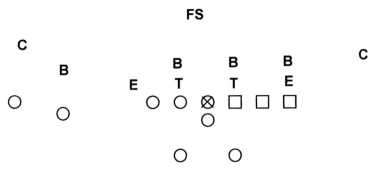

Flexing the tight end helps dictate the duties of the strong side defensive end and outside linebacker.

Diagram 12-5:

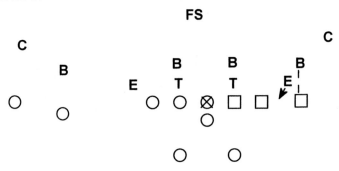

Any time the free safety covers the slot the defense is clearly running one-on-one man coverage. This is a great time to use motion and run "Check Strong".

Diagram 12-6:

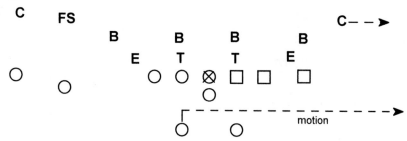

5-2 Defense

Use the slot to take the strong safety away.

Diagram 12-7:

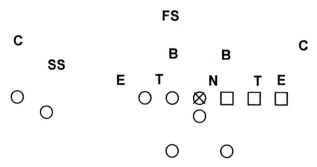

Another defensive alignment change could appear as follows.

Diagram 12-8:

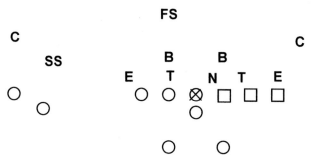

If you want to force the defense to become balanced across the front, simply go to two tight ends. It will also weaken the defense to the strong side if the flanker is placed on the quick side.

Diagram 12-9:

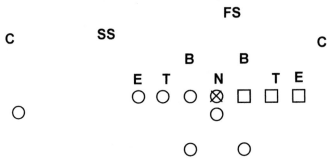

5-3 Defense

Again, because this is a balanced defense it is advantageous to go to the slot formation in an effort to pull out the quick side outside linebacker.

Diagram 12-10:

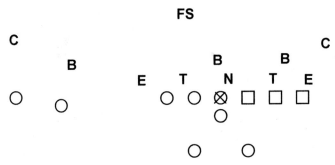

If the free safety takes the slot, it's time to use motion and consider 'Check Strong" possibilities.

Diagram 12-11:

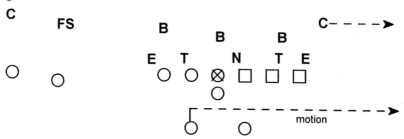

Force the defensive front to balance out by moving the flanker and going to two tight ends.

Diagram 12-12:

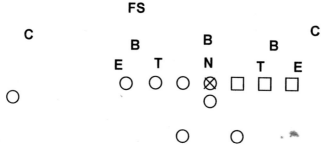

And of course, add 'Check Strong' to the two tight end formation.

Diagram 12-13:

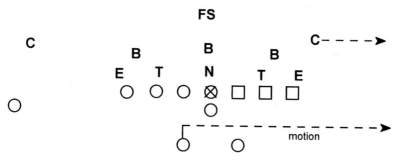

6-2 Defense

You will see this defense a lot whether you realize it or not. This is what 5-2 coaches usually end up doing against the strong side. Look at Diagram 12-7 and Diagram 12-8.

Because it's a balanced defense, use the slot to pull out the defensive end. Now you have an offset 5-2.

Diagram 12-14:

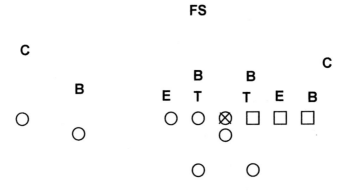

If the free safety goes to the slot, again you know they're playing one-on-one man coverage. Run 'Check Strong' and look at the possibilities.

Diagram 12-15:

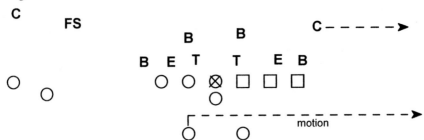

Force the defense to balance out by shifting the flanker and using two tight ends.

Diagram 12-16:

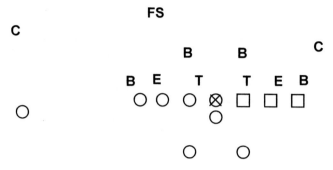

And let's not forget the threats that arise by using 'Check Strong'.

Diagram 12-17:

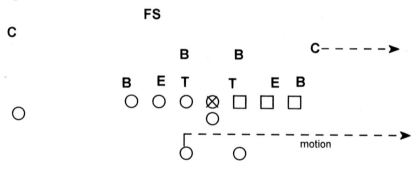

If we want to free up the quick side tight end, leave the flanker to the strong side and run 'Check Strong' with the motion going in the other direction.

Diagram 12-18:

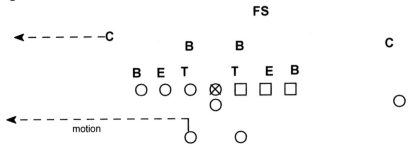

Also, if you think your quick side matches up well, it is possible to run the strong side back in motion and go to 'Check Quick'!

Diagram 12-19:

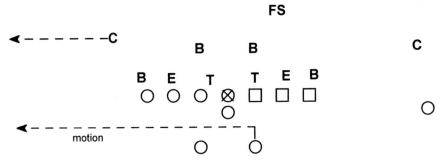

Diagram Review

The following is a short description of which T-Reads plays will and won't work in each diagram listed above.

Review Diagram 12-1:

Available plays: 2,3,4,5

#1 - No, because the strong tackle has an easy release to the backer.
#2 - Yes
#3 - Yes
#4 - Yes
#5 - Yes, because the quick guard can get the tackle.

Review Diagram 12-2:

Available plays: 3,5

#1 - No, because the strong tackle has an easy release to the backer.
#2 - No because the tackle has to offer help to the strong guard.
#3 - Yes
#4 - *No, because the trap rule states to "go away from the closest defensive lineman to the center."
#5 - Yes

Review Diagram 12-3:

Available plays: 2,3,4

#1 - No, because the strong tackle has an easy release to the backer.
#2 - Yes
#3 - Yes
#4 - Yes
#5 - No, the coach should realize the stacked outside backer would out number this point of attack. Go slot and open this up!.

Review Diagram 12-4:

#5 - Yes, because the outside linebacker has been moved out.

Review Diagram 12-5:

#2 - Yes, with a much easier *dive read*.

Review Diagram 12-6:

Available plays: 7(first),2,3

#1 - No, because the strong tackle has an easy release to backer.
#2 - Yes

#3 - Yes
#4 - No possibility due to motion (Check Strong).
#5 - No possibility due to motion (Check Strong).
#6 - No possibility due to motion (Check Strong).
#7 - Yes, always the first choice if no defender "over the top".

Review Diagram 12-7:

Available plays: 2,3

#1 - No, because the strong tackle has an easy release to backer.
#2 - Yes
#3 - Yes
#4 - *No, because the trap rule states to "go away from the closest defensive lineman to the center."
#5 - No, because the quick guard cannot block the tackle.
#6 - No

Review Diagram 12-8:

Available plays: 1,3,5

#1 - Yes
#2 - No, due to defensive tackles alignment.
#3 - Yes
#4 - *No, because the trap rule states to "go away from the closest defensive lineman to the center."
#5 - Yes
#6 - No

Review Diagram 12-9:

Available plays: 2,3,4,6

#1 - No, because of defensive tackle alignment.
#2 - Yes
#3 - Yes

#4 - *No, because the trap rule states to "go away from the closest defensive lineman to the center."
#5 - No, because of defensive tackle alignment.
#6- Yes

Review Diagram 12-10:

Available plays: 1,3,5

#1 - Yes
#2 - No, because of defensive tackle alignment.
#3 - Yes
#4 - *No, because the trap rule states to "go away from the closest defensive lineman to the center."
#5 - Yes
#6 - No

Review Diagram 12-11:

Available plays: 7(first),2,3

#1 - No, because of defensive tackle alignment.
#2 - Yes
#3 - Yes
#4 - No possibility due to motion (Check Strong).
#5 - No possibility due to motion (Check Strong).
#6 - No possibility due to motion (Check Strong).
#7 - Yes, always the first choice if no defenders "over the top."

Review Diagram 12-12:

Available plays: 1,3,4,6

#1 - Yes
#2 - No, due to defensive tackle alignment.
#3 - Yes
#4 - Yes

#5 - No, due to defensive tackle alignment.
#6 - Yes

Review Diagram 12-13:

Available plays: 7(first),1,3

#1 - Yes
#2 - No, due to defensive tackle alignment.
#3 - Yes
#4 - No possibility due to motion (Check Strong).
#5 - No possibility due to motion (Check Strong).
#6 - No possibility due to motion (Check Strong).
#7 - Yes, always the first choice if no defenders "over the top."

Review Diagram 12-14:

Available plays: 1,3,5

#1 - Yes
#2 - No, due to defensive end alignment.
#3 - Yes
#4 - *No, because the trap rule states to "go away from the closest defensive lineman to the center."
#5 - Yes
#6 - No

Review Diagram 12-15:

Available plays: 7(first),2,3

#1 - No, due to defensive end alignment.
#2 - Yes
#3 - Yes, possibly if the quick side linemen can get up to the linebackers.
#4 - No possibility due to motion (Check Strong).
#5 - No possibility due to motion (Check Strong).

#6 - No possibility due to motion (Check Strong).
#7 - Yes, always the first choice if no defenders "over the top."

Review Diagram 12-16:

Available plays: 4,5

#1 - No, due to defensive end alignment.
#2 - No, due to defensive tackle alignment.
#3 - *No, because the trap rule states to "go away from the closest defensive lineman to the center."
#4 - Yes
#5 - Yes
#6 - No, due to defensive end alignment.

Review Diagram 12-17:

Available plays: 7(first),2,3,6

#1 - No, due to defensive end alignment.
#2 - Yes
#3 - Yes
#4 - *No, because the trap rule states to "go away from the closest defensive lineman to the center."
#5 - No, due to defensive end alignment.
#6 - Yes
#7 - Yes, always the first choice if no defenders "over the top."

Review Diagram 12-18:

Available plays: 7(first)2,3

#1 - No, due to defensive end alignment.
#2 - Yes
#3 - Yes
#4 - No possibility due to motion (Check Strong).
#5 - No possibility due to motion (Check Strong).

#6 - No possibility due to motion (Check Strong).
#7 - Yes, always the first choice if no defenders "over the top."

Review Diagram 12-19:

Available plays: 7(first),4,5

#1 - No possibility due to motion (Check Quick).
#2 - No possibility due to motion (Check Quick).
#3 - No possibility due to motion (Check Quick).
#4 - Yes
#5 - Yes
#6 - No, due to defensive end alignment.
#7 - Yes, always the first choice if no defenders "over the top."

This is simply a quick overview of plays and adjustments used against commonly seen defensive fronts. There are always other defensive schemes and variations that you'll have to deal with. We have all been to enough football clinics, and drawn enough plays on napkins to know that the last man with the pen wins. But, in this case, defense only has so many things they can do to stop you. It is your responsibility to know what they are and how to deal with them.

Good Luck!

Obviously the trap can be run in both directions against these alignment, but the T-Reads trap rule consistently offers better angles.

RECOMMENDED READING

The Following are excellent books on the veer offense.

- **The Explosive Veer Offense for Winning Football** by Jim Wacker and Don Morton. Published 1980, Parker Publishing Co., Inc.

- **Attacking Modern Defenses With the Multiple-Formation Veer Offense** by Steve Axman. Published 1978, Parker Publishing. Co., Inc.

In addition, for those coaches wishing to further review the virtues of the flip-flop line, a book has been written on this subject. Even though the actual offense contained does not resemble the veer, specific comments about flip-flopping the offensive line are quite persuasive.

- **The Flip-Flop Offense in High School Football** by Pete Dyer. Published 1967, Parker Publishing Co, Inc.

I consider all of these books fundamental contributors to my growth as an offensive football coach.

PLAYER QUOTES

"It was a lot of fun exploiting the defense. T-Reads was a great weapon because the defense really never knew what we were doing."

Greg Aylsworth
Quarterback

"It's an amazing system for high school athletes. It was so nice to have the decision-making process in the hands of the players. It was awesome!"

Brian Maurer
Quarterback

"Calling the play after the defense is set is a huge advantage. It's like being able to see in the future. It was so much fun!"

Tom Hollenbeck
Quarterback

"T-Reads gave us a distinct advantage over our competition, as we were able to call our offensive plays after the defense was set. By capitalizing on this advantage, T-reads played a vital role in our State Championship in 1994 and helped carry us to the semi-finals in 1995."

Pat Bunting
Strong Tackle

"Coach, just let us run T-Reads and we'll kick their butts."

Chris Walker
Quick Guard
(at halftime of the state semi-finals)

"The T-Reads package was a critical component of our offense. It provided us with the flexibility to assess and attack any part of the defense instantaneously. Dives, options, traps, sweeps...you name it, we could do it, and all at the line of scrimmage. By having trust in the players, our coaches would let us go a whole series without any designated plays…sometimes our entire game plan would be to utilize T-Reads! And to top it off, the system is easy to learn, implement and adjust to the structure of any opponent. I believe that without the flexibility that this system provides, we would not have had the amount of success that we had!"

Todd Ciolek
Running Back

"T-Reads was the backbone of our offense. As a lineman it kept you on your toes, more involved. Eventually, I think it kept our team closer together and really made us more of a cohesive unit. It was a great feeling knowing we could adjust to any defense, and even better knowing we could blow them away!"

Mike Depuy
Strong Guard

ABOUT THE AUTHOR

Bill Hollenbeck lives outside Glen Arbor, Michigan with his wife, Cindy. They have two grown children: Lisa, a recent college graduate, and Tom, presently serving his country in the Armed Services. Bill is an U.S. Air Force veteran having served in Vietnam earning several commendations including the Distinguished Flying Cross.

The author coached high school football in Michigan for 28 years with stints at Chippewa Hills, Mesick, Frankfort, and Maple City Glen Lake. He enjoyed outstanding success during his 19 years at Glen Lake, winning many conference and regional titles, a State Championship in 1994, and the State Runner-Up in 1996. Coach Hollenbeck has received numerous awards, including the Michigan High School Football Coaches Association (MHSFCA) Regional Coach of the Year seven times, MHSFCA Coach of the year in 1994 and 2001, and the Associated Press Coach of the Year in 1989. He was inducted into the Michigan High School Football Coaches Association Hall of Fame in 2001.

In his "spare time" while coaching high school Varsity Football, Coach Hollenbeck has contributed to the growth of youth football in the state of Michigan as well. He was the driving force to originate YMCA Pop Warner football in Northwest Michigan. This association now has over 60 teams and serves over 2,000 youngsters in ten counties. He also spearheaded the origination of a committee for youth football within the MHSFCA, and has served as Regional Director and Youth Football Committee Chairman. In recognition of his efforts, he received the Pete Schmidt Award of Distinction by the Michigan Chapter of the National Football Foundation and College Hall of Fame. Coach Hollenbeck has made a powerful impact on the future of football in the state of Michigan.

Printed in the United States
17589LVS00003B/193-216